IT'S TRUE!

SLEEP MAKES YOU SMARTER

D1102355

WALTHAM FOREST LIBRARIES

028 785 805

BOD

Did you know that frogs are cannibals,
fashion can be fatal and the dinosaurs
never died? Or that redheads were
once burned at the stake as witches?
Find out why rubbish tips are like lasagna,
and how maggots help solve crimes!

Books to make
your brain bulge!
find out all about them on
www.itstrue.com.au

Thalia Kalkipsakis

PICTURES BY Andrew Plant

IT'S TRUE!
SLEEP
MAKES YOU
SMARTER

ALLEN&UNWIN

WALTHAM FOREST	
028785805	
PETERS	08-Sep-2008
£4.99	154.6
M	

All rights reserved. No part of this book may be reproduced
or transmitted in any form or by any means, electronic or mechanical,
including photocopying, recording or by any information storage
and retrieval system, without prior permission in writing from the
publisher. The *Australian Copyright Act 1968* (the Act) allows a maximum
of one chapter or ten per cent of this book, whichever is the greater,
to be photocopied by any educational institution for its educational
purposes provided that the educational institution (or body that
administers it) has given a remuneration notice to Copyright Agency
Limited (CAL) under the Act.

Allen & Unwin
83 Alexander Street
Crows Nest NSW 2065
Australia
Phone: (61 2) 8425 0100
Fax: (61 2) 9906 2218
Email: info@allenandunwin.com
Web: www.allenandunwin.com

National Library of Australia
Cataloguing-in-Publication entry:

Kalkipsakis, Thalia.
It's true! sleep makes you smarter.
Bibliography.
Includes index.
ISBN 978 174114 862 6.
1. Sleep – Juvenile literature. 2. Dreams – Juvenile literature.
I. Title. (Series: It's true; 25)
154.6

Series, cover and text design by Ruth Grüner
Cover photographs: Chip Simons/Getty Images (girl) and
Allen Wallace/Photolibrary (brain)
Set in 12.5pt Minion by Ruth Grüner
Printed by McPherson's Printing Group

1 3 5 7 9 10 8 6 4 2

**Teaching notes for the It's True! series are available
on the website: www.itstrue.com.au**

Contents

WHY SLEEP?

1

EXTREME BURNOUT 1

2

ENEMIES OF SLEEP 10

3

CYCLING THROUGH THE NIGHT 21

4

TICK TOCK BODY CLOCK 33

5

**CROC DREAMS
AND SLOTH SLUMBERS** 41

6

MYSTERiOUS DREAMS 51

7

WHAT iS A DREAM? 58

8

NOW YOU'RE THE EXPERT 72

Quiz 83

Thanks 86

Where to find out more 87

Index 88

WHY SLEEP?

Tiny cows the size of mice might seem weird to you, but they mean a lot to me. If I dream of them stampeding across my bedroom floor, that means I'm too busy and need some chillout time. It's true!

In learning to understand my mini-cow dream, I've discovered loads about what happens when we sleep.

I read about 'early birds' and 'night owls', and birds that sleep as they fly. I laughed at the crazy things that sleep scientists get up to with warm water and feathers, and the crazy positions of astronauts snoozing in their space shuttle. I discovered why we often dream of being frozen, unable to move, and why sleepwalking can be embarrassing – *really* embarrassing . . .

Come on, let's snuggle up and visit the amazing world of sleep and dreams.

1

Extreme burnout

Randy's record

Did you know that if you miss out on too much sleep you will die? It's true! If you stay awake for a long, long time, your brain hits meltdown and your body packs up. It's death by extreme burnout.

The unofficial world record for staying awake is 11 days, and it's held by high-school student Randy Gardner. Randy asked two of his friends to stop him falling asleep. He also had help from TV and radio reporters, a sleep researcher and a doctor called in by Randy's worried parents.

What happened? First of all, staying awake for too

long made Randy REALLY GRUMPY. Then his brain started to scramble. On day 4, he thought a street sign was really a person. On day 6, he began to speak very slo-o-o-wly and had trouble naming common objects. On day 9, he couldn't finish sentences (by the end of the sentence, he would forget how he'd started). On day 10, Randy started believing that a radio announcer was out to get him and thought he saw a forest in the next room.

YOU'RE tired! I've been balancing on one leg, for years!

In fact, he went a bit crazy.

Eventually, after he'd broken the previous world record, Randy was told to go to sleep. Experiments that keep people awake for dangerously long periods are always stopped before the patients hit meltdown.

Rats aren't so well cared for.

Ruined rats

When rats are kept from sleeping, they die within three weeks. (That's sooner than if they'd been allowed to sleep but were given no food.)

They get really thin. But that's not because they stop eating – quite the opposite. Even though these rats are gulping down food, their bodies can't process it in the normal way. They turn into skinny eating machines.

On top of that, their little bodies lose more heat than normal, which makes them weak. This means that they need even more food to stay at a healthy temperature.

Towards the end, these exhausted rats develop ulcers (open sores full of pus) on the soles of their paws and their tails. That's a sign that their immune systems are failing.

OK, so I'm a little sleepy, but it's a real "all you can eat" diet!!

Normally rats' bodies can ward off bacteria (germs), but without sleep this protection fails. They'll get blood poisoning and then die.

Temperature meltdown, gooey ulcers, and blood poisoning . . . That's what extreme lack of sleep does for you.

RATS' RIGHTS

Experiments to discover more about sleep have caused some rats to suffer and die. Many people believe it's wrong to harm animals, even if it helps humans. Some also argue that tests on animal bodies are not relevant to human bodies.

These days, many researchers try to minimise the pain and suffering they cause to animals. They aim to find different ways of testing their ideas.

STAY UP LATE . . . AND PAY

Staying up late can be bad for you. It's true!

If you need nine hours shut-eye and you only get seven one night, then you'll create a 'sleep debt' of two hours, a bit like owing money to a bank. The next night you'll need about 11 hours – your normal nine, plus your 'payback' sleep of two hours.

People who keep on clocking up sleep debts start to show all the icky symptoms of burnout:

☼ They are more likely to get sick.

☼ They don't process glucose (a kind of sugar) well and may even develop an illness called diabetes.

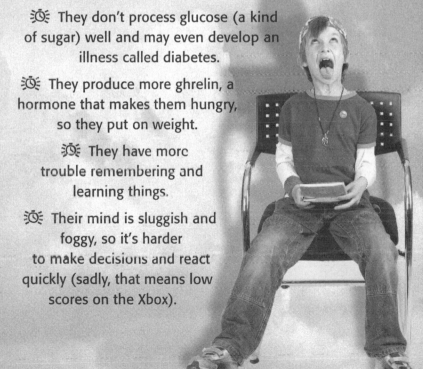

☼ They produce more ghrelin, a hormone that makes them hungry, so they put on weight.

☼ They have more trouble remembering and learning things.

☼ Their mind is sluggish and foggy, so it's harder to make decisions and react quickly (sadly, that means low scores on the Xbox).

Microsleeps and mega mistakes

Luckily we don't need to lie awake at night, worrying about gooey ulcers and going crazy. If you're really short of sleep, your body just takes over. The longer you keep yourself awake, the more adenosine builds up in your brain. (Adenosine is a chemical that makes you drowsy.) The more adenosine there is in your brain, the more difficult it is to (yawn) stay aw-a-a . . .[1]

In fact, you could argue that Randy Gardner didn't really stay awake for 11 days. (That's why his record is unofficial.) There's a good chance that he had secret microsleeps – sleeps lasting just a second or two that other people might not notice. Only sleep-deprived people (and maybe lab rats) have them.

Imagine that you stay up all night at a sleepover. Next day you go to school feeling a bit light-headed and sit down at your desk. You've got a maths test. The teacher is droning on about decimals or algebra . . .

BAM . . . microsleep.

[1] Want to know how coffee keeps people awake? It contains caffeine, which blocks adenosine's effect on nerve endings.

You can't remember what you're meant to be doing, and your brain is tired and foggy. Blink. If only you could remember what you learned last week . . .

Bombing out in a test is bad news for you, but it's not a big drama for other people. It's a different scene when sleepy adults drive a car or run nuclear power plants. Then microsleeps can cause BIG problems. Lack of sleep has been blamed for some massive disasters (see box next page).

Zombie drivers

Closer to home, experts think that sleepy drivers probably cause quite a few road accidents. In fact, people who are very short of sleep do worse in problem-solving and co-ordination tests than people who are drunk. For this reason, drug companies are scrambling to invent pills that stop the effects of sleep deprivation. If they are successful, they could make a lot of money.

DROWSY DISASTERS

In 1989 the *Exxon Valdez* oil tanker
hit a reef near Alaska. It spilled 41 million litres
(11 million gallons) of oil, killing thousands of animals
(otters, seals, orcas and probably 250 000 seabirds).
What went wrong? It seems that the first mate, who was
in command of the ship at the time of the accident,
was sleep-deprived. He'd had only six hours on his bunk
in the last 48 hours.

In 1986, a nuclear reactor in Chernobyl exploded, killing
31 people. The radioactive fallout since then has caused
illness, death and hardship for many more people,
maybe 2.5 million. The explosion happened at
1.23 a.m. – a time when workers' bodies were
telling them to sleep.

Wow – big bucks and big mistakes. That's a lot of
fuss about sleep.

Everyone should make sure they get enough sleep.
Easy, right?

Wrong. As you'll see in the next chapter, falling
asleep (and staying that way) isn't always as easy as
it sounds.

Teacher: Sally, you can't sleep in my class!

Sally: If you were a bit quieter I could.

POD OFF

Ever wanted to put your head on your desk and nod off? You should! After 10–20 minutes snoozing, you'll feel happier and more alert, and do better at school.

Some schools in Japan have scheduled 15 minutes of nap time after lunch. Now the students are getting higher test scores. Naps are making them smarter!

'Nap salons' have also opened up in big cities around the world – special shops where adults can take a nap. For just a few bucks, they can snuggle up inside a 'sleep pod' – an artificial cocoon perfect for slumber. The pods are even fitted with an alarm clock – but it's bring your own teddy!

Perhaps there should be sleep pods on oil tankers and in nuclear power plants too.

9

2

Enemies of sleep

Lots of things can go wrong with sleep – there are over 70 different kinds of sleep disorders. Here are some of the more common (or more interesting) ones:

Sheep but no sleep

Have you ever had trouble going to sleep, or going back to sleep after waking in the night? That's called **insomnia** (in-som-nee-a). It feels as if your body has forgotten how to sleep.

With most people, the reason is clear – they're excited, in a different bed (maybe on holiday), or there's too much noise outside. Something is disrupting their sleep routine.

People who don't fall asleep when they first lie down might have to wait 90 minutes before they can. That's the magical length of a sleep cycle. At the end of a cycle, their brain is back in the 'starting position' for sleep.

Insomnia that happens all the time for no clear reason can be diagnosed as a sleep disorder. It's more common in older people.

Snooze, snooze, choke!

Try holding your breath and counting to 15 . . . yikes! Bet you're out of breath now.

NIGHT TIME . . . UNPLUGGED

Here's a nightmare for you – imagine life without electricity. No lights, no TV and (gasp) no computer games. Aaaaaaaauuuuuugh!

Electricity doesn't only allow us to use TVs and computers. It also affects our sleep.

For people who live without electric lighting, bedtime is more or less at sundown – up to 12 hours before sunrise.

With so much 'down' time, people don't sleep right through the night. Instead, their sleep is split into two blocks. In between is a period (sometimes called 'watch') of quiet rest and reflection.

In the past, people used this time to pray, think about the meaning of a dream, or to talk with another family member.

These days, people who wake during the night are diagnosed with insomnia. But maybe they are just sleeping (and waking up) naturally.

That's exactly what happens to people with **sleep apnea** (ap-nee-a) – sometimes hundreds of times a night.

It's most common in people who are over 65 or obese (or both). The extra fat and loss of muscle tone means that their airway collapses when they lie down and fall asleep.

They are snoring happily,[2] then everything goes quiet . . . suddenly, snort, gulp, they wake up for a moment, start breathing again and go back to sleep. When they wake up the next morning, they have no idea what has been happening. They're not sure why they feel tired and grumpy after a full night's sleep.

The sudden drop in oxygen each time they stop breathing is bad news. It causes high blood pressure (their blood pushing harder against the walls of their arteries), which makes them more likely to have a heart attack or stroke. They're also more likely to have a car accident because they are so tired.

[2] Not all people who snore have sleep apnea. Long pauses between the snores (when the breathing stops) is a sign of sleep apnea.

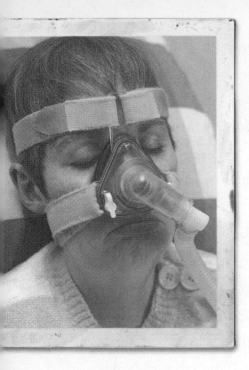

Some apnea sufferers stop breathing in their sleep, and never start again.

Luckily, there is a treatment – an oxygen pump in the bed! People with sleep apnea have to wear a special breathing mask each time they sleep.

Galactic snores

Ever checked out the back of your mouth in a mirror? You would have seen your uvula (the dangly bit), the back of your tongue and the top parts of your throat. In a snore, all these throaty bits vibrate, making a not-so-musical snoring sound.

When you lie down and relax, your airway gets smaller. In people who snore, it gets so small that the air has to squash past. That's when the noisy vibrating starts.

Gravity might also play a part. We know this because some astronauts stop snoring in space! Without the normal tug of gravity their airway stays wide open, and each breath has a clear path.

Don't tell Mum. She might want to send Dad off into outer space!

Wriggly and restless

Do you ever find it hard to sit still? Maybe when the lunch bell is due? Imagine if you felt like that in bed!

Some people do.

They have **restless leg syndrome**. It is a prickly, tingly feeling on their arms and legs – like ants crawling on them.

The only way to stop the creepy feeling is to move their arms and legs – not so helpful when they're trying to sleep.

Marvin Lambini-
sleepwalker,
restless legs sufferer,
night marathon runner.

Snoring through dinner . . .

Ladies and gentlemen, welcome to the Narcolepsy Sufferers Associ....

Someone with **narcolepsy** can fall asleep anywhere, any time, without warning. They might be in the middle of eating dinner when (zzzz) their head droops and bingo! they are asleep, sometimes for up to 30 minutes. (Hmmm, with peas stuck up their nose?)

We're not sure what causes narcolepsy. But it seems that something is going wrong in how the brain signals when to sleep and when to dream.

...ation Dinner.

THUMP!   THUMP!

Some animals are prone to narcolepsy – horses,
bulls and some breeds of dog. Scientists are studying
these animals to find a cure for narcolepsy in humans.

. . . or falling down laughing

People with narcolepsy might also suffer from another
disorder called **cataplexy**. During a cataplectic attack
they collapse and lose all control of their muscles,
as if they were dreaming. But they're wide awake!
Cataplectic attacks can happen when the sufferer feels
a strong emotion like fear or joy. Simply hearing a joke
can cause a collapse.

Walking, talking and ---ing
in your sleep

Some kids walk and talk in their sleep. They might
wander around the house with their eyes open, or
mumble garbled words, but still be fast asleep.

    Sleepwalking usually occurs in the first part of
the night. Scientists think that it happens when the

sections of the brain for staying awake and falling asleep are not working together properly.

Most sleepwalkers and talkers remember nothing about it in the morning. But a few are rudely awakened. These are the ones who think they're walking to the toilet. Sadly, they end up sitting on the couch or a coffee table instead . . . woops!

Thinking he was going to the toilet, sleep-walking pet-shop owner Warren made a fatal mistake.

Vampire invasion

You might be sharing your bed with real-life vampires.

Bedbugs love the taste of human blood. Their flat round bodies (about 4 millimetres long) are perfect for hiding in tiny cracks near your bed.

SLEEPING SICKNESS . . .

Sleeping sickness is a disease that affects 36 countries in Africa and is passed on by the tsetse fly. It has two stages. In the first stage, you feel weak, headachey and feverish. If you aren't treated with the right medicine, you'll go to the second stage, in which you can't sleep at night and you can't *stop* sleeping in the daytime. If you aren't cured, you'll die.

. . . AND NOT-SLEEPING SICKNESS

Another disease, called fatal familial insomnia (FFI) affects the part of your brain that regulates sleep. It takes seven to 36 months to kill you. At first you have trouble sleeping. Then, after a few months, hallucinations and panic attacks start. Soon you can't sleep at all and get super skinny. In the final stage, your brain scrambles and you're even too tired to talk.

Luckily, FFI is extremely rare. Only people from 28 families worldwide have a chance of getting it.

When you lie
down, the bedbugs
sense warmth
from your
body and the
carbon dioxide
you breathe out.
'Yum, fresh, warm
blood,' they think. Like
mosquitoes, they have special
saliva that stops your blood clotting while they suck.

AAAARG!
BED BUGS!

After a feed, bedbugs leave a row of tiny bites
on your body and a matching row of blood spots on
your sheets. Creepy!

Bedbugs used to be a normal part of life. With the
use of strong insect sprays in the 1940s and 1950s, they
almost disappeared. But these days our insect sprays
aren't as strong (better for us and for the environment),
so bedbugs are making a comeback.

3

Cycling through the night

Remember that feeling?

You're in a deep sleep, peaceful and relaxed.

Or maybe you're dreaming of fighting a dragon, or escaping from the army of cockroaches invading your house.

Either way, you're pretty busy.

Bzzz . . .

Then something wakes you up. Ouch.

It's hard to think. Your eyes are glued shut.

Being woken before you're ready feels so unnatural that it almost hurts. It's like going to bed before you've seen the end of a movie. Something very important hasn't finished yet . . . It's your own personal TV show, and you're missing out on the grand climax!

TV in bed

'Lights out, lie down,' calls your dad. It's time to go to sleep.

When you first drift into sleep, you sometimes have a floating or falling feeling. (That's why we talk about 'falling' asleep.) You might also get flashes of memories or vague glimpses of dream images.

From here, you begin a sleep cycle that lasts about 90 minutes. During this cycle, you flip between two different kinds of sleep. (Think of it as a 90-minute TV show with ad breaks.)

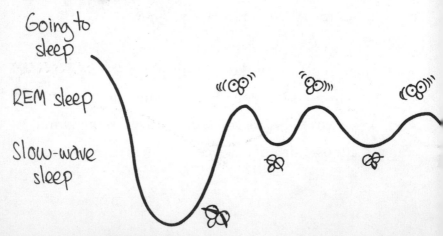

Going to sleep

REM sleep

Slow-wave sleep

❶ REM sleep (REM stands for 'rapid eye movements') is when you're most likely to dream. This is the TV show.

❷ Slow-wave sleep has no eye movements and less chance of dreaming. This is the ad break.

In a normal night, you pass through about five of these cycles (so, five TV shows). But these cycles aren't exactly the same. As the night goes on, they change. How they change gives us some clues about what is happening.

REM channel surfing

Waking up

CUDDLE UP COSY

In traditional societies, families slept together on skins or mats, sometimes on a wooden platform, but often on the ground.

For a long time, beds were a sign of wealth. In ancient Egypt, King Tutankhamen had a bed made of gold and ivory. During the Roman Empire, rich people had beds decorated with precious metals and jewels.

The ancient Romans also had a 'table bed' – a place to eat while lying down! These beds had space for three people. The middle was seen as the best spot.

In the sixteenth and seventeenth centuries, mattresses were put on top of a lattice made from ropes. These ropes needed to be tightened now and again – perhaps this was the origin of the saying 'Sleep tight'.

Poor families would often have many children to a room, and many children to a bed. They'd sleep 'top to tail', with in-between ones having their heads at the foot of the bed, to save space.

Slow-wave sleep . . .

At the start of the night, the 'ad breaks' (slow-wave phases) are long. So your first 90-minute TV show for the night has lots of strung-out ads, with only short bursts of the show.

Slow-wave sleep is the peaceful, slow phase of sleep; the low point in your sleep cycle. Your breathing and heartbeats are slow and regular, and your body temperature drops. This is when your body does nuts-and-bolts repairs – growth hormones are released, your immune system is actively warding off germs, and most of your brain has a rest.[3]

As the night continues, you go through more slow-wave then REM sleep cycles. Your body has some solid time in deep sleep and the important rest and repairs are under control. Now the ad breaks are shorter, and the TV show really gets going.

[3] A tiny section of brain cells starts working only during this phase. It's activated by higher temperatures, which is why you can feel sleepy when you're in a hot bath or lying in the sun.

MUM'S NEVER-FAIL
ALARM CLOCK

You still hear sounds in your sleep. The 'hearing' part of your brain registers noise as it does when you are awake. (It may even incorporate that sound into a dream. Have you ever had a swimming dream while it's raining?)

But it doesn't stop there. A 'sleep hearing' part of your brain decides whether the sound should wake you up. That's why mothers wake so easily with a tiny wail from their baby, but can sleep soundly through the noise of a nearby train station.

Honey, I think the baby coughed!

Revved-up REMs

As the slow-wave phases get shorter, your REM phases (when you dream) get longer. Your last dream for the night is usually the most detailed and crazy, too.

If you are always woken by an alarm, this is the phase of sleep that you will miss part of.

During REM sleep, you're at the high point in your sleep cycle. Your breathing and your heartbeat speed up and become irregular, just as they do when you're awake. Your brain is also active, which is strange considering you are unconscious. Your muscles, on the other hand, go floppy. (Just as well. If that didn't happen, you might spread your wings and fly in bed, or kiss your pillow, dreaming about your tennis coach!)

The muscle block doesn't affect eye muscles, so your eyes still move about under your eyelids as you look at things in your dream. (Remember what REM stands for?)

Ever watched your dog or cat sleeping? Notice the twitching and eye movements while they dream.

Sometimes you can tell what their dream is about, just from watching their face and listening to them breathe. Catch that rabbit, Jock!

Yeah, I had a great night's sleep, but my eyes are exhausted!

How much sleep do you need?

Some people need more time in bed than others. It depends on age, body type, and much more . . .

THE YOUNGER THE SLEEPiER

Babies need heaps of sleep, but kids need less and grown-ups least of all. Here are the average sleep needs per day for different ages.

Newborn babies ▶ 16 hours
Children 1–12 ▶ 10–12 hours
Teenagers ▶ 8½–10 hours
Grown-ups ▶ 7–9 hours

THE THiNNER THE SLEEPiER

Metabolism (met-tab-o-lizm) is the conversion of food to energy and new body cells. If you have a fast metabolism (you eat lots of food and still stay slim), you probably need more sleep than average. If you have a slow metabolism (you don't eat much but you're big), then you may need less sleep than other people.

Yep, all that metabolising is sure wearing me out!

Why does metabolism affect sleep needs? Well, in the process of converting food, your body also creates

THE EJECTOR BED

What kinds of beds can you think of? Air beds, folding beds, sofa beds, trundle beds, camping beds, hammocks, box beds, four-posters with curtains, electric hospital beds, beds that fold into the wall . . . Are there others? What kind would you most like to have?

In October 1855, *Scientific American* magazine ran an ad for the 'Ejector Bed', designed to 'cure the sin of sloth'. When the sleeper 'recklessly dared to sleep beyond his allotted period of rest' an alarm would sound. If the person stayed in bed, a side rail would slide down and the bed would tilt – throwing the person onto the floor!

But I AM a sloth!

THE SIN O'SLOTH EJECTOR BED

'free radicals', chemicals that can damage and even kill cells. Sleep gives your body a chance to make some repairs. The more damage there is, the more sleep time you need to fix it.

CHANGE ME, CHANGE MY SLEEP

Your sleep needs can vary a lot. Change anything (except maybe your underwear) and your sleep needs will change.

GET SICK: We already know that lack of sleep can suppress your immune system. It works the other way too. When your body is fighting infection, you'll need more sleep.

GET ACTIVE: Remember adenosine? It's the chemical that makes you drowsy when you stay awake for ages. Guess what else produces adenosine: exercise. When you do more running around or sport than normal, you also need more sleep. (But fit people who play a lot of sport or go often to the gym generally need less sleep than unfit people, so sleep after exercise for them is a bit like savings in the bank.)

OFTEN STAY UP LATE: If you get less sleep than you need, you begin to build up a 'sleep debt'. In other words, you'll need extra sleep as 'catch-up'. (Yep, sleeping in at weekends is actually *good* for you!)

GROW: When you're growing, you'll be hungrier and need more sleep. It all gets back to metabolism. When you are growing, there are more chemical reactions inside you, and more damage to cells.

START CHANGING: We all know about the wobbly bits and hairy bits that appear when you reach puberty. Of course, all those extra chemical reactions will mean you need more repair time at night. But there's something else about puberty that can affect your sleep.

It's not a bomb, but there's something pretty powerful ticking away inside you right now . . .

4

Tick tock body clock

Guess what? You have your very own alarm clock, inside your brain. (So you can throw your 'normal' alarm clock out the window and watch time fly!)

Your internal 'clock' is a complex system that controls the 'high points' and 'low points' every 24 hours of your heartbeat, body temperature and many other things. It also determines when you feel most alert (around 10 a.m. for most people) and when you are most likely to sleep.

During Randy Gardner's 11-day non-sleeping ordeal, he found it most difficult to stay awake in the early hours of the morning (roughly 2 to 5 a.m.). That was exactly when Randy's internal clock was most urgently telling him to sleep.

Your internal clock is so powerful that even when single cells are removed from your body, they continue working on a 24-hour cycle (more or less).

In fact, even when people are locked away for days, without clocks, windows or any indication of time (sounds fun, hey?), they continue to follow this cycle.

However, they don't stay exactly in sync with the world outside. People who are locked away (in what scientists call 'free-running' time) usually end up on a sleep-wake cycle slightly longer than 24 hours.

It's not usually a problem. Your internal clock has clever ways of staying synchronised with outside events. Many things, like exercise and meal times, will keep your internal clock in line with the 24-hour system.

SARDINES IN SPACE

Astronauts don't sleep very well, but that's not because they are worried about safety. In space, the sun rises and sets every 90 minutes and that disrupts their internal clock. (To find out how, read page 36.) They have to sleep in strange places, too. In space there is no 'up', so they can't lie down to sleep!

A bunk bed can sleep two people as normal (top and bottom bunk). A third person can sleep on the underside of the bottom bunk, facing the floor! There's even room for a fourth person to sleep upright on a bunk stuck vertically to the end of the other two.

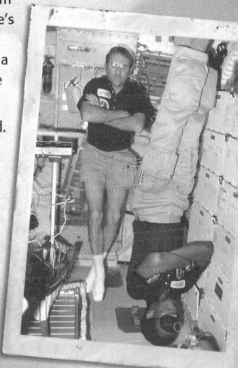

Each bed is a padded board. It feels soft because there is no gravity pulling the astronauts into the board. A sleeping bag is strapped to each one. Astronauts have to zip themselves in to avoid floating away.

Wonder what happens to the drool?

Sun sync

There's another cycle that's even more powerful than your internal clock. It's the biggest and hottest thing that you'll ever see.

Yes, it's the sun.

The pineal gland in the middle of your brain is affected by light. Light during the day is like an Off switch for your pineal gland. It stops producing a special hormone called melatonin, that makes you feel sleepy. After sunset, the switch flicks to 'On' and melatonin is produced again . . . time for bed.

Not surprisingly, people who are totally blind sometimes have trouble sleeping. Since light can't affect their pineal gland, they're stuck in a 'free-running' sleep-wake cycle that doesn't fit with everyone else's daily body rhythms.

Melatonin rules over the *timing* of your sleep. Adenosine, which we heard about in chapter 1, is involved in the *amount* of sleep you need. Together (with some other complex 'switches' in your brain) they help you fall asleep and stay that way.

YOUR BODY CLOCK

1 a.m. Most likely time for pregnant women to go into labour. Immune cells at their peak.

2–4 a.m. Deepest sleep and lowest body temperature. Growth hormone at its highest level. In those not asleep (but they should be), car accidents and industrial accidents most likely.

6–7 a.m. Heart rate and blood pressure begin to surge. Melatonin levels begin to fall. Risk of heart attack and stroke is highest. Hay fever symptoms are worst.

8 a.m. Immune cells at their lowest daytime level. Now is when you're most likely to do a poo.

10 a.m. Zap! A time of high alertness.

1 p.m. Small drop in body temperature and alertness. Time for a nap.

2–6 p.m. Time for ballet and footy – coordination and reflexes at their best. Body temperature, pulse rate and blood pressure at peak.

9 p.m. Pain threshold is lowest (i.e. you're least able to take pain). Melatonin begins to be released – it's nearly time for bed.

Clever, hey? Your internal clock is reset every night to keep you in tune with the world around you.

But light isn't the only thing that can re-set your internal clock.

Wobbly bits and the internal clock

If you really had an internal clock, you wouldn't hear a simple 'tick tock'. It would sound more like a whole room full of clocks. Some, like your sleep-wake cycle, would go dong every 24 hours. Others would go dang every 90 minutes or so (at the end of a sleep cycle). One or two would go off once in a lifetime.

When you reach puberty (dingdingdingding), hormones are released that start off all the growing and changes. Some scientists now believe that puberty also re-sets your sleep-wake body clock. There seems to be a delay in melatonin release at night during puberty. Since melatonin makes you feel sleepy, a delay in melatonin release will make your natural bedtime slightly later. Maybe that's why you (or your big brother or sister) are up till all hours . . . (Or perhaps it's

because of artificial lighting from TV and computers
– no kidding, it could be.)

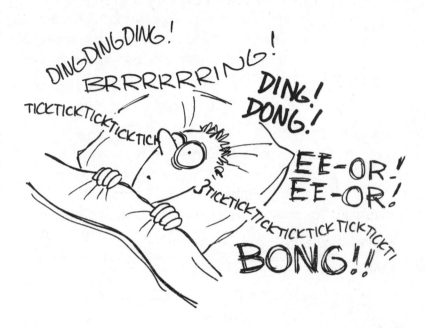

On top of that, we already know that during
puberty you need more sleep because you're growing
and metabolising. No wonder all these alarms are going
off. One of them is a real alarm clock, waking you up
each morning!

WHAT A HOOT

Are you an 'early bird' or a 'night owl'?

Some experts think they know why some people feel best in the morning and others are most awake late at night. They say it's linked with body temperature.

Over a day, everyone's core body temperature changes by about 1 degree Celsius. We feel most alert when our body temperature is high.

Early birds have a rapid increase in body temperature when they first wake up. That's why they jump out of bed, singing like larks, 'Calloo, callay, what shall we do today?' Night owls have a gradual increase in body temperature, so it takes them longer to wake up. 'Whassat? Go 'way, leave me alone . . .'

Everyone has a peak in body temperature each evening. After that, the early birds' temperature falls quickly – making them drowsy and ready for bed.

In night owls, body temperature doesn't drop so quickly after their evening peak. They feel more alert than they have all day. 'Hoot,' say the owls. 'Why go to bed when the fun has just begun?'

5

Croc dreams and sloth slumbers

What's the time, Mr Wolf?

Even though animals can't tell the time, they do have an internal clock. Just like yours, their bodies go through highs and lows over a given time (usually a day, but sometimes less).

They all show low points when they're less active and don't pay attention to what's happening around them. But does that mean they sleep?

The answer is 'No'. Sleep as we know it is not something that all other animals do.

'Simple' animals like insects, worms, fish and

frogs have inactive, 'dormant' periods, but things like hormone release and fighting off infection aren't happening when they rest.[4] There is a chance that they have their own kind of sleep, though. When scientists pester fruit flies during their 'dormant' phase,[5] the flies then have more dormant time the following day – probably catching up on their lost 'fly sleep'.

When you take a look at more complex animals, sleep starts to get even more interesting.

[4] Hibernation in bears and skunks is similar to dormancy – the animal's body temperature drops and it uses very little energy through the winter. But hibernation is not sleep.

[5] Hmmm, how do you annoy a fly?

Did the dinosaurs dream?

Which animal has sleep cycles most like your own?

A Turtles

B Mice

C Seagulls

The answer is 'B': mice. That's because they're mammals like us, meaning they have warm blood and their babies drink milk from the mother.

Turtles and seagulls both sleep. But they're not mammals and they don't have sleep cycles like ours. Turtles are reptiles and their sleep is only slow-wave – they don't have REM sleep, so they probably don't dream. The same is true for lizards and snakes.

But some larger reptiles, like crocodiles probably do dream, in very short bursts. ('Probably' because scientists disagree about this.)

Do you think dinosaurs dreamed? If crocodiles do, dinosaurs might have as well. They certainly wouldn't dream the way we do, with stories that we can remember, but imagine if they did! Would they have nightmares about raptors, or dream of being the biggest and brainiest brachiosaur on the block? What do you think?

What about birds? Baby birds do dream, just after they have hatched. Adult birds hardly dream at all! Their dreams are only a few seconds long, and are the only time when they sleep and close both eyes. The rest of their time asleep, they keep one eye open for danger.

Lion lunch?

If you thought a lion wanted to eat you, you'd probably run away. Or maybe you would hide. You definitely wouldn't lie down and go to sleep, would you?

If you did sleep, then you wouldn't have much chance of waking up again.

Gulp.

It might sound silly, but that's the exact worry for

lots of animals every time they sleep. The fact that they still sleep, even when this makes them more vulnerable to predators, is yet another clue that sleep is vital for health.

To stay safe from foxes or other predators looking for dinner, lots of animals sleep in weird and wonderful places.

Orang-utans gather leaves each night to prepare a soft mattress for themselves in the trees. They wrap their fingers and toes around the branches so they don't fall during the night. Sloths lock their claws around a branch and sleep upside down. The golden dormouse carefully balances on a tree branch to sleep. If the branch quivers, the mouse wakes up, ready to run.

Mountain goats don't sleep in trees, they sleep on narrow rocky ledges, leaning against the cliff.

Seals can sleep on land or on water. Body fat and air inside their bodies help keep them afloat in the water so they can breathe.

Many animals sleep in a curled-up position with their nose and tail touching. A fox will use its bushy tail as a pillow. Birds will tuck their beak into the feathers above the wing. These postures help to conserve body heat, keeping the animals warm while sleeping.

Birds have all sorts of cool ways to sleep. Wrens have claws that lock around a branch as they squat down on it. That way, they don't fall out of their tree as they doze.

Flamingoes, herons and many other birds can sleep with one leg tucked up and not lose their balance.

Elf owls will sleep inside a cactus, once the woodpeckers who made the hole have left.

Swifts can even sleep while they fly. On long migrations, when they fly to warmer weather, they have microsleeps rather than landing to sleep.

Duck for cover

Some kinds of ducks sleep in groups to stay safe. The ducks on the edge of the group sleep with their outward eye open, watching for hungry predators.

It doesn't sound very restful, but the duck's brain makes it possible. The brain is made up of a left and right section (called hemispheres). When these ducks nod off, they only sleep with one side of their brain at a

THE GREAT BIG ELEPHANT MOVES SO SLOW

Which animals do you think need the most sleep and which ones need the least? Take a guess.

Do intelligent animals need more sleep?

Do slow, inactive ones like koalas need less?

Neither of these is true. It's size that determines how much sleep an animal needs. The bigger the animal, the less sleep it needs. So elephants and giraffes are *awake* most of the time; rats and cats spend most of their day sleeping. Humans are in between.

Why is this so? The simple answer is 'metabolism'. Small animals metabolise fast, so they need more catch-up and repair time.

time – the side that is linked to their open eye.

This is probably why adult birds have so little REM sleep. When they close both eyes to dream, they can't 'keep an eye out' for danger.

Dolphin dreaming

Dolphins also sleep with one half of their brain at a time. Their brains swap sides during each sleep cycle, so that both hemispheres have a chance to rest. But that's not because of their eyes, it's because of their lungs. They are 'conscious breathers' and need half of their brain awake enough to swim to the surface for air. When scientists give them drugs that put both sides of their brain to sleep at the same time, they stay underwater and stop breathing.

Of all the mammals, dolphins spend the least time in REM sleep. In fact, we're not sure they dream at all. When you remember how active your brain becomes during a dream, then this makes sense. Perhaps if a dolphin started to dream, it would be too busy to remember to breathe.

Horsy habits

Horses need sleep – and they can do it standing up! Their knees lock straight and so use very little energy. If danger looms, they can gallop off in an instant.

But they still sleep lying down some of the time.

Guess which kind of sleep they're in then . . . That's it – REM sleep. Remember how your muscles go floppy while you dream? If horses started to dream while standing up, their loss of muscle tone would make them fall over.

Even though lying down to sleep makes it harder for them to escape from danger, horses still lie down sometimes to dream.

Hmm . . . We know that sleep is important because of what happens when you don't sleep (still remember the rats?). But lots of animals put themselves in danger just so they can *dream*. So what's so important about dreaming? To find out, read on!

6

Mysterious dreams

Gods and doctors?

Once upon a time, I, Chuang-tzu, dreamed I was a butterfly . . . Now I do not know whether I was a man dreaming I was a butterfly, or whether I am a butterfly now dreaming that I am a man.

Over 2000 years ago, in 350 BCE, Chuang-tzu was asking a question that still fascinates people today. Are dreams a reflection of the real world? Or are they a link to something mystical or other-worldly?

Many people in ancient cultures believed that some dreams came from God. The founder of Islam, the Prophet Mohammed, received inspiration and guidance through dreams. Jews believed that angels could appear in dreams as messengers from God. The ancient Egyptians, Greeks, Romans and Chinese all had rituals such as fasting, bathing, saying prayers and burning incense before going to sleep. They hoped to receive answers or cures to sickness as they dreamed. In one Chinese province, people would even sleep on graves!

Hello? Hello? I was just having a nap!

FIFTEEN IN THE BED
AND THE LITTLE ONE SAID . . .

The Great Bed of Ware was built in England around 1590. It is 326 centimetres wide by 338 centimetres long – big enough to sleep 15 people. (To give you an idea of how big that is, a king-size bed today is about 183 centimetres wide by 204 centimetres long.) The Great Bed of Ware has a post at each corner, nearly 3 metres high, with curtains on three sides and a big carved headboard.

The Chinese also believed that your soul could leave your body while you slept and visit the spirits of the dead. People tried not to wake up a sleeper too quickly in case their soul didn't have time to return to their body. The ancient Greeks had a similar idea, and the Indians even believed that if you wake up too quickly, you could die.

The Indians thought that dreams could predict the future. A dream from early in the night would come true in a year's time. A dream from the middle of the night might not come true for eight months and dreams from the end of the night were coming true now.

Dreams weren't mystical for everyone, though. Some of the ancient Greeks thought they were connected to the waking world. Hippocrates, a famous doctor, used dreams to help diagnose disease.

And then I dreamed that the alarm rang and I woke up – and it was true!

Wow, amazing dude!

Galen, who lived 300 years after Hippocrates, also used dreams to work out what was wrong with his patients. He even operated on them because of what he understood from their dreams!

Would you let a doctor operate on you because of a dream? Would you use a machine that was invented in a dream? What about reading a book that was inspired by a dream?

Dreams that changed the world

Take a look at the clothes you're wearing, at a sleeve or a hem. Can you see the stitching?

If it wasn't for a dream, you would be wearing very different clothes!

In the 1840s, an Englishman called Elias Howe was trying to invent a mechanical sewing machine, but he couldn't make it work. Then he dreamed he was going to be eaten by cannibals. The cannibals all held spears with eye-shaped holes in their tips. Bingo! That was the exact detail that Howe needed to make his sewing machine work.

Another riddle was solved in chemistry when Freidrich von Kekule dreamed of a snake with its tail in its mouth. He had been trying to understand how a molecule called benzene held itself together. Once he dreamed of the snake, he solved the riddle – the benzene molecule is in the shape of a ring!

Dreams like this don't happen only to the scientists or inventors.

'Yesterday, all my troubles seemed so far away . . .'

Do you know that song?

Believe it or not, Paul McCartney dreamed the tune to 'Yesterday'. He describes tumbling out of bed and playing the tune: 'It was all just there, a complete thing.

REAL-LIFE SLEEPING BEAUTY

In August 1941, when Elaine Esposito was six,
she was put under an anaesthetic for an operation.
She never woke up. Elaine stayed in a coma until she died
in 1978 – an amazing 37 years and 111 days later.

During that time she slept some of the time, and was
unconscious the rest of the time. She became known
as 'Sleeping Beauty'.

Maybe all she needed was a kiss . . .

I couldn't believe it; it came too easy. In fact, I didn't believe I'd written it.'

Rolling Stones guitarist Keith Richards dreamed the riff for '(I Can't Get No) Satisfaction'.

Artists like Salvador Dali and William Blake have depicted their dreams in their paintings and drawings. Writer Robert Louis Stevenson said he dreamed a scene from *The Strange Case of Dr Jekyll and Mr Hyde* when he was trying to come up with a story idea.

Charlotte Brontë, the author of *Jane Eyre*, used dreams to understand feelings, such as how it might feel to take a drug called opium, even though she would never try opium in her waking life.

Imagine if dreams like this happened to you!

They can. See chapter 8 for ways to find inspiration in a dream.

FLUFFY PILLOWS . . . OR NOT

Pillows, like beds, have been a sign of wealth. Most poor people didn't have one!

Some pillows aren't meant to be comfy. They are sewn and dyed so elaborately that they become works of art.

A traditional Chinese pillow is a hard box for your head. Not soft and cosy at all.

7

What is a dream?

Snorkel while you snooze

Have you ever played a trick on your friends at a
slumber party? One trick goes like this: wait until
someone is asleep, then gently put their hand in a bowl
of warm water. If the trick works – so the story goes –
then your friend will wet the bed.

Even if that doesn't happen, you might still
have some effect. Maybe your friend will dream of
snorkelling or scuba diving . . .

Believe it or not, that's one of the experiments that
sleep scientists have used to discover what happens
when we dream.

Dream debt

It all began over 50 years ago, when scientists first worked out how to tell for sure when someone is in REM sleep (dream-sleep). Ever since then, they have been sticking wires on people's heads and watching them dream (and doing strange things with bowls of water, or with feathers). They also do experiments with people before and after sleep – for example, asking them to watch violent movies or take a drug to stop dreams happening.[6]

They found out that people who are stopped from entering the REM phase and only allowed to have slow-wave sleep one night will slip straight into a long phase of REM sleep the next.

Just as having a sleep debt is bad for your body, we now know that having a 'dream debt' is bad for your mind. But why? Why do we dream? And what if you can't remember any dreams?

---

[6] They only do this with volunteers – people who have agreed to be part of an experiment.

Most experts say that you don't need to remember your dreams for them to do their job. They find it harder to agree about *why* we dream.

Why do we dream?

You are in your old house, and you are flying. Not too high, but you're definitely skimming over the floor without touching it. It feels great. Why can't you move around like this all the time?

You're in the kitchen, but you don't want to be there. You want to go outside. Squirm, struggle . . . you try to

get to the door, but something is stopping you. Something
is pulling you back.

You struggle some more . . . you thump your fist on
the kitchen table . . . you're not sure what is holding you
back. Aaaaggh!

Then, suddenly, you are outside and flying. Free.

Your dreaming time is the only time you'll ever know
how it feels to fly like a bird. But dreams are also the
only time you might ever know utter terror.

The dream we just described is not a real one. But
flying, struggling, being in a house, and feeling free
or frustrated are often
part of our dreams.
Funnily enough,
your dreams will
usually have you as
the star!

NIGEL-
LORD
OF THE
UNIVERSE

So what does it all mean? If it means nothing, then why is there a story? If it does mean something, why is it so hard to understand?

The answer is 'Nobody knows, tiddley-pom'. But there are lots of theories.

[1] CHUCK OUT THE JUNK

Some scientists say that dreams are meaningless. For them, dreams are flashes of random brain activity while we sleep, and the fact that we sometimes remember dreams is just an accident. In fact, some say that we dream to forget about useless memories, or to discharge (let go of) strong emotions. Otherwise, they say, our brain might become cluttered and confused.[7]

The 'Chuck Out the Junk' crowd might say that the layout of your old house is a useless memory, so it gets 'lost' in our sample dream. Perhaps you've been feeling frustrated during the day, and the flying dream helps to

---

[7] It's like a bedroom that's never tidied. The longer you leave it, the harder it is to find anything you need. (Yes, Mum . . .)

release that frustration before it makes you crazy.

They might also say that the feeling of being held back is an example of the real world becoming part of the dream. That common feeling of being stuck or paralysed comes from the muscle block (the floppiness) that happens during REM sleep.

[2] PUSH-UPS FOR YOUR BRAIN

Another lot of scientists think of dreams as a way of developing the mind. They focus on newborn animals.

For example, a baby platypus dreams for hours while a dolphin hardly dreams at all. The scientists' idea is that dream time is linked to how helpless the animals are at birth. A newborn platypus can't see, keep itself warm or find food on its own. It just lies around like a blob. Perhaps dreams help its mind develop. A dolphin is a mammal, like the platypus, but it has to swim as soon as it is born, so its brain is already highly developed.

Human babies are more than a blob, but they are just about as helpless at birth as the baby platypus, and they spend about half of their sleep time dreaming. (For adults, it's about a quarter, or even less.)

Just like the 'Chuck Out the Junk' crowd, these scientists might say that our flying dream is meaningless. It is just exercise for our brain, and it doesn't matter what the actual images are.

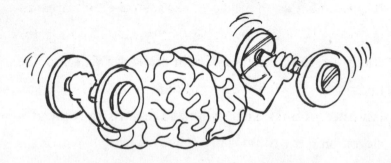

64

Imagine you are two years old and someone has just stolen your hot dog.

What do you do?

Maybe you thump the thief, or maybe you start crying. Either way, you do whatever comes naturally.

What if the same thing happened to you now you're older?

You don't want to get into trouble. You also want people to like you. So you swallow the anger and try to get your hot dog back in a 'polite' way. According to our third theory of dreams, the anger then comes back into your sleep in some way.

Lots of people, not just psychiatrists, think that dreams reveal hidden secrets – thoughts and feelings the dreamers don't even realise they have. But dreams are tricky because they are full of symbols – things that stand for something else. So, in our sample dream, the kitchen table might be a symbol for your hot dog (see the connection?). That's why you feel frustrated and angry near it.

Looking for secret codes in dreams is very popular. People use this method to understand themselves better and to solve problems (such as how to invent the sewing machine!). See chapter 8 for ways to 'cook up' your own Eureka dream.

[4] DREAMS ARE LiKE CLOUDS

Have you ever stared at a fluffy cloud and seen something else – a face, a rabbit, a three-headed giant snowman?

Some scientists think that dreams are exactly like seeing faces in clouds. Your dreams start as flashes of random brain activity, as meaningless as clouds. (That's why dreams are so weird.) Then, they say, your forebrain tries to make sense of these flashes. However, as it's your brain trying to link them and make a story, the dream can still reveal something about you.

So the 'Clouds' idea is similar to the 'Secret Codes' idea. The meaning of our flying dream would depend on what all the dream images suggest to you when you recall them after waking.

FAMOUS DREAM EXPERTS

In 1900, Sigmund Freud published *The Interpretation of Dreams*, a book that made him and the 'Secret Codes' idea famous.

Carl Jung took the 'Secret Codes' idea even further, and added some ideas of his own. He said that certain symbols mean the same for everyone.

- A king and queen is a symbol for your parents.
- A house is a symbol for your body or your mind.
- Flying means you feel free and confident.
- Falling means you are worried you might fail.

Some people argue that they got it all wrong, but Freud and Jung are still the most famous dream experts.

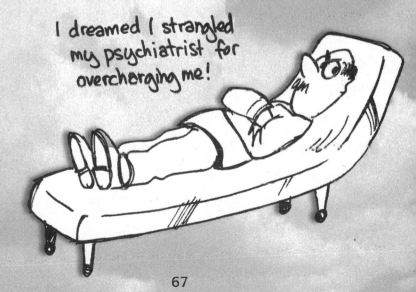

I dreamed I strangled my psychiatrist for overcharging me!

[5] REPLAY & REMEMBER

What happens when you watch repeats of a TV show over and over? Or when you replay a favourite movie on DVD? Do you notice different things, or maybe more little details?

The same thing happens while you sleep. During REM sleep (and sometimes during slow-wave sleep), your brain signals match the ones you had during the day. Some people say that your brain is replaying recent experiences, and choosing details to remember.

It seems that only some kinds of experiences are 'saved' as you dream. Your memory of history facts or spelling doesn't get better as you sleep. But a host of other kinds of memory do improve with sleep. One is 'spatial memory' – e.g. remembering the path home from school. Another is 'procedural memory' – e.g. playing a video game or learning how to ride a bike. It's as if your dreaming brain lets you practise these skills in your sleep.

Other scientists go even further and suggest that your sleeping brain is also finding new ways of looking at the world. It's not just replaying your life, it's also processing the events and working out how to match them with something you learned in the more distant past.

It's a bit like saving new files onto a computer. When you load a new file (a new experience) onto your brain, it opens up old files that are similar or relevant. Then, as you dream, the files are joined together or put in a logical order before they are re-saved.

This kind of shuffling and re-saving, say some scientists, helps us find new ways of looking at the world. A problem that seems impossible while we're awake is replayed with a fresh perspective as we dream. This is how science explains the mysterious dreams in chapter 6.

Experts can't agree on exactly which part of the sleep cycle helps you sort through and store your memories. Some say that the final bout of REM sleep is most important (remember that your dreams get longer in the last part of the night). Others say that swapping between slow-wave and REM sleep is important to memory, as if your brain talks to itself and works out which memories to save.

Slow-wave brain: Salutations, brain, did you acquire any new insights today?

REM brain: Yeah, man! You bet! It was so, like . . . amaaaaazing!

So, let's take one last look at our flying dream.

The 'Replay & Remember' experts might say that something you need to remember now is linked to something you learned at your old house. Perhaps flying is your brain's concept of how it felt when you first learned to walk, and now you are learning to rollerblade. Your dreaming brain is searching back through memories of your past and adding a new experience to your collection.

YOUR INNER TODDLER

What is your first memory? The time you wet your pants at kinder? The time you decided you could fly? Your first memory is likely to be of an unusual event from age two or three.

Some scientists have found a change in the way we dream from around two. That's the start of our 'critical period', when we start remembering the key things in our life, and trying to make sense of the world. We do it by connecting things mentally.

For instance, as a child you might have noticed that *If I pack up my building blocks, Mum smiles at me.* Then, as you dreamed, the image of your building blocks was linked to the good feeling of a smile from your mum.

The next time you feel the same way (perhaps you get a smile from your teacher), your brain will dream of the experience and link it with building blocks. You might dream that your classroom topples down like a tower of blocks. That's why dreams are so strange, say these scientists. Your dreaming brain is packed full of pictures and feelings that are linked to events from your past.

8

Now you're the expert

OK, enough talk about scientists and experts (they never seem to agree about anything anyway)! Now it's your turn to become a dream expert. You've heard all the ideas about why we dream. Why not try them out yourself?

Man, I had the strangest dream! I was a thousand times bigger and only had two legs!

Ugh! Sounds like a nightmare!

You'll need a notebook and a pen. And . . . ah yes, you'll need a dream.

Recipe for a dream

Do you want to be a millionaire? Become a movie star? Invent time travel?

Well . . . er, um . . . sorry, dreams can't help you do those things. Not unless you're already earning big bucks or studying acting, or unless you are the smartest scientist in the world.

The good news is that dreams of inspiration (sometimes called Eureka dreams) can help you see your own life and your own problems in fresh and amazing ways.

INGREDIENTS

❶ A specific problem or issue that is important to you. It might be 'What's a good way to present my history assignment?' or 'Should I quit choir?' or 'How can I feel happier at school?'

❷ Time thinking about the subject.

Spend time writing, drawing or talking about it. Don't try to think of a solution now – leave that for the dream.

METHOD

Now it's time to let go – when you're getting ready for bed, put away the picture or writing on the topic and tell yourself that it's time for your dreaming mind to take over. Imagine yourself waking up with an answer or fresh perspective on the topic. Then, simply, go to sleep.

If you wake from a dream, it might have the answer you're after. But remember, that might not be obvious. Who would have thought that cannibals and spears would help someone to invent the sewing machine?

Dream-catching

Don't move! To remember a dream, try to wake up slowly in the morning, without moving or opening your eyes. Now recall what you were just dreaming about. Get as much detail as you can.

- What colours, smells, objects, people, animals were there?
- What was the 'story' of the dream?
- When is the dream from: your past or present? Maybe it's about something in the future?
- How did you move? Were you stuck or could you fly? Did you move normally?
- Where did the dream happen – in a place you know? Did you jump from one place to another?
- Most important of all, try to remember how you felt during the dream.

Now it's time to write the dream down. If you already keep a diary, you can use that (some people like to write about their days on one side of an open spread, and about their dreams on the other side). Otherwise, just use a notebook or exercise book. You might like to draw a picture of something from your dream.

When you're recalling the feelings in the dream, also write about how you feel now, after waking up. Is it different from how you felt before you went to sleep?

Now you have your very own dream to study . . . but what on earth does it mean?

Putting the puzzle pieces together

Now you're ready for the fun part. Try to link something in your dream with the real world.

- A feeling: you felt trapped and angry like at the picnic last week.
- An object: you dreamed that your flute suddenly grew to be as tall as you.
- A person or an animal: your mum grew horns and said 'moo'.
- A place: a caravan park? The middle of the ocean?

Maybe you can't see any links at all: the dream was really weird!

If you can't see any links, then maybe you agree with the 'Chuck Out the Junk!' crowd, or the 'Push-Ups for Your Brain' idea. Maybe your dreams just don't have meaning.

If you can see a link, then you have a clue about why your mind created this dream. From here, you can try to find more links. You could write down your link in the middle of a piece of paper and try to connect it to something else in the dream. Look at your dream 'pictures' and try to imagine what else they could mean. Sometimes it's fun to talk about your dream with someone who knows you well.

Now you can choose your dream theory, based on what you see in your dream:

- 🤔 Did your dream release a feeling or a useless memory?
- 🤔 Did you do something in your dream that you really want to do in real life?
- 🤔 Did the dream show you a new way of looking at a problem, or help you better understand the world?

How did you go? Maybe your dream still makes no sense, or made you worry about something? Let's take one last look at dreams.

Bad breath and frozen chickens

Dreams can be great fun, or they can make you feel terrible. The things you've learned in this book can help with the bad dreams.

Scientists might argue about why we dream, but they all agree that dreams come from your mind. That huge, scaly monster with nine heads that's chasing you? It's your own unique invention. That cute guy or girl who gave you a frozen chicken? They're your special fantasy (actually the frozen chicken is too).

Dreams might feel real, especially when you're having one, but they're not.

If you dream about something in the future, it's probably about your hopes and fears for what might happen. If you dream that your parents die, if you dream that you're going to fail a test, it has everything to do with how you feel about your parents and tests and nothing to do with what's really going to happen.

Since dreams come from your mind, they're just as likely to make a mistake as you are while you're awake.

That's even more true when emotions get involved. If you are worried about something during the day, then there's a big chance that you're going to dream of it at night. You might even have a nightmare about it.

If you're worried that you have bad breath, and then dream that you start breathing fire and set alight your school bus, it doesn't mean that you really have bad breath (nor does it mean you were a dragon in

a past life). It's just something that worries you enough during the day to make itself important to your dream mind. If there's something on your mind, then it might make its way into your dreams.

This is true for good dreams, too. (Pity!) If you dream that the tall guy from basketball training gave you a medal, it doesn't mean that he's going to do it in real life. It just means that you want to be a success in basketball! It's OK to enjoy dreams like this, but don't forget that they are exactly the same as a wish.

The same is true when you dream that you see someone who is dead or in another country. Some people believe that these kinds of dreams are real (it's called astral projection). Actually, it's more likely that something reminded you of the person, and this is why you had the dream.

NIGHTMARES

Nightmares are most common in children who are around three, but they can happen to anyone. They usually happen in the second half of the night, during REM sleep. This is when you have your longest and weirdest dreams.

Night terrors are different. They happen in the first half of the night, during deep sleep. During a night terror, children start screaming and thrashing about, even though they're still fast asleep. As with sleepwalking and talking, they'll remember nothing in the morning.

Nightmares . . . nick off!

If you keep having the same nightmare or dreaming over and over again about something bad that happened to you, try changing what happens inside your dream.

While you're still awake, close your eyes and think through the nightmare. But instead of letting the nasty thing happen, change it in some way – however you like. Imagine the monster disappearing, or your attacker suddenly shrinking to nothing.

If that doesn't stop the nightmare coming back, try thinking it through again and tell yourself to look at your hands at a certain point in the dream. The next time you have the dream, looking at your hands will help you remember that you are dreaming and can take control even while you sleep.

Phew! What a lot of things happen every time you sleep – blood-sucking vampires, crazy TV shows with ad breaks and secret dream codes.

Good night, sleep tight.
Don't let the bedbugs bite.

SLEEP QUIZ

**1 The world record for staying awake
is unofficial because:**

(a) the official time-keeper fell asleep ☐
(b) the record keeps being broken by party animals ☐
(c) the record holder probably had microsleeps ☐
(d) the record-holder died before he went to sleep ☐

2 If you have a nap at school, you'll:

(a) feel happier and more alert ☐
(b) do better at school ☐ (c) probably be woken by
an angry teacher ☐ (d) all of the above ☐

3 Bedbugs feed on:

(a) drool ☐ (b) nightmares ☐ (c) blood ☐
(d) the crusty bits in the corner of your eye ☐

4 Snoring:

(a) is nature's alarm clock ☐ (b) stops in space ☐
(c) is a sign that you're a deep sleeper ☐
(d) helps you make friends ☐

5 During REM sleep, your brain:

(a) goes floppy ☐ (b) is active, as it is when you
are awake ☐ (c) shuts down completely ☐
(d) replays songs from the band REM ☐

6 A good time to do a maths assignment is:

(a) never (what a silly question!) ☐ (b) midnight, the night before it's due ☐ (c) on the school bus ☐ (d) mid-morning ☐

7 Human sleep is similar to sleep of:

(a) foxes ☐ (b) seagulls ☐ (c) fruit flies ☐ (d) dinosaurs ☐

8 To stay safe, the golden dormouse sleeps:

(a) hidden behind doors ☐ (b) while it's flying ☐ (c) with one eye open ☐ (d) balancing on a branch ☐

9 Horses lie down to sleep because:

(a) they need to dream ☐ (b) they're trying to hide ☐ (c) standing up wastes energy ☐ (d) everyone else does and they want to be cool ☐

10 Dreams:

(a) make you wet the bed ☐ (b) only happen to toddlers ☐ (c) are important for a healthy mind ☐ (d) are messages from another world ☐

11 Nightmares:

(a) give you bad breath ☐ (b) predict the future ☐ (c) are a sleeping disorder ☐ (d) are created from your mind ☐

ANSWERS: 1c 2d 3c 4b 5b 6d 7a 8d 9a 10c 11d

THALIA KALKIPSAKIS used to think that sleep was a waste of time. As a kid, she much preferred to read (under the covers with a torch) through the night hours.

These days, Thalia absolutely adores sleep, but her two kids are excellent alarm clocks and never let her lie abed. Her husband keeps her awake with superb coffee.

Thalia is a great believer in letting ideas brew overnight – some of her tricky writing problems have been solved this way. Now and then, Thalia even writes in her sleep. Maybe this book is all a dream . . .

ANDREW PLANT says, 'When I was a kid, I dreamed of being an artist. Twenty years later, I was. Spoooky!!!

'Like many artists, I'm a night owl and do my best pictures when I stay up late, much to the annoyance of my early-bird wife. I hope you find them a hoot.'

Thanks

Thanks to the eternally tired neuroscientists and sleep experts who have dedicated their careers to studying sleep – specifically J. Allan Hobson, Jerome M. Siegel and Jonathan Winson. A special thanks to Sarah Brenan who made the editing process a joy.

Thalia Kalkipsakis

The publishers would like to thank istockphoto.com and the photographs named for images appearing on the following pages: Ken Babione (clouds used throughout text); pages i and 43 Bob Kupbens (gila monster); pages v and 45 David Kahn (sea lions); pages vii, 14 and 35 Stefan Klein (photo frame); page viii kreicher (pig); page 3 Fabian Guignard (rat); page 5 Chris Schmidt (boy playing computer game); page 12 Adam Lukasiewycz (lightbulb); page 14 Andres Balcazar (mask); page 24 step2626 (piglets); page 28 Björn Kindler (polar bears); page 37 owe (alarm clock); page 40 Tan Kian Khoon (owl); page 45 Gregory Van Raalte (sloth), Matthias Mueller (mouse) and Don Wilkie (alpaca); page 47 Laura Frenkel (flamingoes); page 48 Adam Booth (koala); page 71 bratan007 (wooden blocks); page 74 Bobbie Osborne (gorilla); page 82 Jaap Uilhoorn (hand). Thanks also to NASA for the photographs of the sleeping astronauts on pages vii and 35.

Where to find out more

Books

(you may have to buy from Amazon) www.amazon.com:

M. J. Abadie, *Teen Dream Power*, Bindu Books, Vermont, 2003

Robert Matero, *Animals Asleep*, Milbrook Press, Connecticut, 2000

Trudee Romanek, *The Most Interesting Book You'll Ever Read About Sleep*, Kids Can Press, Toronto, 2002

Websites

Neuroscience for Kids:
- http://faculty.washington.edu/chudler/sleep.html

Wake Up Australia! About sleep health in Australia:
- www.sleepaus.on.net/wakeup.pdf

Sleep on the BBC:
- www.bbc.co.uk/science/humanbody/sleep

On sleep disorders, and more:
- www.talkaboutsleep.com

The USA National Sleep Foundation:
- www.sleepfoundation.org/

On sleep in space – NASA for Kids and Kidspace (from the Canadian Space Agency):
- www.nasa.gov/audience/forkids/home/index.html
- www.space.gc.ca/asc/eng/kidspace/kidspace.asp

For teachers
- http://dreamtalk.hypermart.net/teachers/
- www.asdreams.org/idxeducation.htm

index

accidents 7, 8, 13, 35
adenosine 6, 31, 36
animal dreams 43,
  44, 64
animal sleep 41–50
  birds 46–7
  dinosaurs 44
  dolphins 49, 64
  foxes 46
  goats 46
  golden dormouse
  45
  horses 50
  mammals 43
  orang-utangs 45
  platypus 64
  reptiles 43
  seals 46
  sloths 45

bedbugs 18–20
Blake, William 56
body clock 33–40
brain hemispheres
  47, 49
Brönte, Charlotte 56

caffeine 6
cataplexy 17
Chernobyl nuclear
  accident 8

Dali, Salvador 56
dormancy 42

dreams 51–82
  ancient beliefs
  51–4
  critical period 71
  Eureka dreams
  54–7, 73–4
  helping memory
  68–71
  interpreting 76–8
  predicting the
  future 79
  reason for 58–71
  recalling 75–6
  symbols in 65–7

early birds 40
Exxon Valdez oil
  tanker 8
eyes during sleep 23,
  27–8

fatal familial
  insomnia 19
Freud, Sigmund 67

Gardner, Randy 1–2,
  33–4

hibernation 42
Howe, Elias 54

insomnia 10–11

Jung, Carl 67

light, effect on sleep
  36, 40

McCartney, Paul 55
melatonin 36, 37, 38
metabolism 29, 32,
  48
microsleeps 6–8

napping 9
narcolepsy 16
night owls 38
night terrors 81
nightmares 78–82

pillows 57
puberty 32, 39

rats 3–4
REM sleep 23, 27–8,
  see also dreams
restless leg syndrome
  15
Richards, Keith 56

sewing machine 54
sleep apnea 11, 13–14
sleep debt 5
sleep deprivation 1–9
sleep disorders 10–20
sleeping sickness 19
sleepwalking 17–18
slow-wave sleep 25–6
snoring 13, 14–15
space 15, 35

von Kekule, Fredrich
  55